TAKE A BREATH, MOMMY!

You Got this… Because Gods Got You!

DEDICATION

This book is lovingly dedicated to my mother.

I am the mother I am today because of her. When God gave us Ruby L. Bradley, He gave us more than enough. She was a strong, faithful woman who carried so much with grace. As a single mother, she made sure we were always taken care of. Even on the days when her body was tired and she was battling illness, she still showed up for us.

We didn't always have everything we wanted, but we always had everything we needed. Her love, sacrifice, and strength laid the foundation for the woman and mother I am today. The most important part of that foundation was the way she taught me to be firmly rooted in Christ.

Though she is no longer with me, she continues to be a giant in my life. Her legacy lives on in everything I do, and I carry her with me in every step of this journey.

To my amazing husband, Delvin, and our beautiful children (Arianna, Caitlyn, Deja, Alaynna & Oscar), thank you for being my daily reminder of God's goodness. You are my why, my motivation, and my greatest joy. Through every challenge and every triumph, you give my life meaning and purpose.

I also want to extend my heartfelt thanks to my pastors, Pastor Levie and Gwen Taylor, Jr., for your continued support and for consistently pouring into us as parents. Your guidance and prayers have been a blessing to our family.

To the mothers who have been forerunners in my life, those who have loved, supported, advised, and stood beside me, I may not name you all, but you know who you are. Your presence has strengthened me in more ways than I can express, and I am forever grateful.

To the four women who continue to keep me grounded: my Aunt Cleo S. Scott, Charlene Adger, Glenda Lemelle and Geneva House Darden, thank you for always pushing me to be better. Your love, wisdom, and encouragement mean more than words can say.

It is my prayer that I can be that same source of love, strength, and support for someone else.

With love and gratitude,

Shamarian

Foreword

To every mom, mommy, mama, mother; however, you are known and loved… this is for you.

Motherhood is beautiful, but let's be honest, it can also be overwhelming. The responsibilities, the expectations, the constant pouring out… can leave you feeling exhausted, unseen, and in need of just a moment to breathe.

This devotional was created with you in mind.

My journey into motherhood didn't turn out as I once imagined. A hysterectomy at the age of 25 meant I could not physically have children, even though my heart longed for them. Yet God, in His faithfulness, fulfilled that desire through marriage and adoption. Today, I am the mother of four beautiful girls and one amazing boy.

And while motherhood has been one of my greatest blessings, it has also come with real challenges.

I didn't know that my son would be diagnosed with ADHD and Autism. Some days are filled with meetings, tantrums, difficult school calls, and doctor appointments, all while running a business and working a full-time job. There are moments when it feels like too much.

But I decided… to lean on God.

His Word has anchored me in chaos, strengthened me in weakness, and reminded me that I am never alone.

Take A Breath, Mommy is more than a devotional—it's a lifeline.

It is a daily reminder that even in your busiest, hardest, and most overwhelming moments, you can pause, breathe, and find strength in God's presence.

Each day is designed to meet you right where you are. And through the "Mouth Moments," you are not only encouraged to read the truth, but to declare it. Because there is power in your words. When you begin to speak what God has said, your strength is renewed, your mind is reset, and your heart is encouraged.

Momma, you are stronger than you feel, more capable than you think, and deeply loved by God.

So, take a breath…

And let Him meet you right here.

With love,
Shamarian

Breathe... God is with you.

TABLE OF CONTENTS

Take a Breath, Mommy

TABLE OF CONTENTS (continued)

Breathe... God is with you.

How to Use This Devotional

This devotional was created to give you a moment to pause, breathe, and reconnect with God in the middle of your day.

There is no pressure here, just presence.

Each day is designed to guide you through a simple, meaningful rhythm:

1. Read the Scripture
Start with God's Word. Let it speak to your heart and establish the tone for your day.

2. Read the Devotional
Take a moment to reflect on the message. Allow it to meet you right where you are.

3. Pray
Pause and talk to God. Release your thoughts, your concerns, and your heart to Him.

4. Declare the Mouth Moment
Speak the truth of God's Word over your life. Even if you don't feel it yet, declare it anyway.

5. Release and Reflect
Let go of what you've been carrying. Use the Mommy Moment to journal, process, and breathe.

Mouth Moments are short, faith-filled declarations designed to align your words with what God has already spoken. There is power in your words. When you begin to speak truth daily, your mind is renewed, your heart is strengthened, and your faith grows.

Take your time. Come as you are. And remember…

Speak it. Believe it. Breathe again.

Breathe... God is with you.

Take a Breath, Mommy

Day 1: Strength for Today

Scripture: *"I can do all things through Christ who strengthens me." – Philippians 4:13*

Hey Mommy… pause for a moment.

Some days begin before the sun rises. Little feet. Little cries. Big responsibilities. And somehow, before you've even brushed your teeth, you already feel behind.

There are moments when the thought crosses your mind: "I can't do this today." And truthfully, on your own, you can't. But you were never meant to.

This verse isn't about being "Supermom." It's about surrender. Paul wrote these words from a place of hardship, not comfort. He understood something powerful: strength doesn't come from having everything together; it comes from staying connected to Christ.

God is not asking you to carry motherhood in your own ability. He is offering His strength in exchange for your weakness. When your patience runs thin… He strengthens you. When you feel unseen… He strengthens you. When you're exhausted yet still show up… He strengthens you.

And sometimes His strength doesn't look like energy. Sometimes it looks like grace after you've messed up. Sometimes it looks like choosing not to quit. You don't need strength for next year. You need strength for today.

And today… He's got you. Take one step. Whisper a prayer. Lean in.   His strength is enough.

Prayer: Lord, I feel tired in ways I can't always explain. Be my strength today. Help me rely on You instead of trying to carry everything myself. Amen.

Mouth Moment
I can do all things through Christ.
He is the source of my strength.

Breathe… God is with you.

Mommy Moment: Where do I feel the weakest right now? What would it look like to invite Christ into that specific area today?

Day 2: His Grace is Sufficient

Scripture: *"My grace is sufficient for you, for my power is made perfect in weakness." – 2 Corinthians 12:9*

Mom's guilt is loud, isn't it?

You replay the moment you lost patience. The tone you wish you could take back. The thing you forgot. The thing you didn't do well enough. Motherhood has a way of highlighting every flaw. But here's the truth: God's grace fills every gap.

Paul begged God to remove his weakness. Instead, God gave him grace. Not because weaknesses were good, but because grace is greater. Grace covers the sharp words. Grace covers the tired responses. Grace covers the days that didn't go as planned.

You don't have to be a perfect mom to be a good one. God never called you to perfection. He called you to dependence. Your weaknesses are not proof that you're failing. They are proof that you need Him, and that's exactly where His power shows up best.

Instead of beating yourself up today, let grace wrap around you. You are learning. You are growing. You are trying. And His grace? It is more than enough.

Prayer: Father, help me accept Your grace. When I fall short, remind me that You are not disappointed in me. Teach me to rest in Your mercy. In Jesus' name, Amen.

Mouth Moment
God's grace is sufficient for me.
His power is made perfect
in my weakness.

Breathe... God is with you.

Mommy Moment: What mistake or moment am I still carrying guilt over? Can I release it to God right now?

Day 3: You Are Not Alone

Scripture: *"Fear not, for I am with you; be not dismayed, for I am your God."* – *Isaiah 41:10*

There are lonely moments in motherhood that no one really talks about. The middle-of-the-night feedings. The long days without adult conversation. The silent doubts you don't say out loud. Even in a house full of people, you can feel alone. But God's promise is simple and powerful: *I am with you.*

Not only on good days or when you pray perfectly. Right now, He is with you in the rocking chair, waiting in the carpool line, or in the chaos of the kitchen and the messy emotions. He sees your hidden efforts, your mental burden, and the tears you quickly wipe away. Though the world may feel like it doesn't see you, God always does. And you are never alone in your mothering.

Take a breath. He is near!

Prayer: Lord, when loneliness creeps in, remind me that You are right here. Help me feel Your nearness today. In Jesus' name, Amen.

Mouth Moment
I will not fear… God is with me.
I am strengthened and upheld by Him.

Breathe… God is with you.

Mommy Moment: When do I feel the most alone in motherhood? How might it change my perspective to remember God is present in that moment?

____

____

____

____

____

____

____

____

____

____

____

____

____

____

Day 4: Rest in Him

Scripture: *"Come to me, all you who are weary and burdened, and I will give you rest." – Matthew 11:28*

Mommy… you are allowed to rest. Not when everything is finished. Not when the house is perfect. Not when everyone else is happy. **NOW!**

The world glorifies being busy. But Jesus invites rest. Rest is not laziness. It is obedience. You give so much. Emotionally, physically, spiritually. And if you never refill, you'll run dry. Jesus knew that. That's why He said, "Come to Me."

Rest might look like five quiet minutes in the bathroom. A short walk outside. Turning worship music on while you cook. Going to bed earlier instead of scrolling. Rest is choosing to stop striving and start trusting. You are not the Savior of your home. Jesus is.

So, breathe. Release the pressure. Sit with Him for a moment. He restores what motherhood drains.

Prayer: Jesus, I am tired. Teach me how to rest in You without guilt. Restore my body, my mind, and my heart. In Jesus' name, Amen.

Mouth Moment
I come to God for rest today.
My burdens are lifted, and my soul is restored.

Mommy Moment: What keeps me from resting? What small act of rest can I intentionally choose today?

____

____

____

____

____

____

____

____

____

____

____

____

____

____

____

Day 5: Wisdom for the Journey

Scripture: *"If any of you lacks wisdom, let him ask of God..." – James 1:5*

Momma,

Motherhood is a daily series of decisions. How should I discipline this? Should I say yes or no? Am I handling this the right way? Did I respond correctly? There's no manual for raising your specific child. But there is a God who knows them better than you ever could.

And He says: Ask. Not Google. Not comparison. Not panic. **Ask Him!**

God is never annoyed by your questions. He is generous with wisdom. He sees the bigger picture, including the heart issues, the future, and the personality He placed within your child. You don't have to have all the answers. You just need to know the One who does.

Before reacting today, pause and pray. Even if it's a whisper: "Lord, give me wisdom right now." He will guide your tone. He will guide your timing. He will guide your decisions.

You are not figuring this out alone!

Prayer: Father, I need Your wisdom daily. Guide my words, my discipline, and my decisions. Help me lead my children with clarity and love. Amen.

Mouth Moment
God gives me wisdom freely.
I have clarity and direction for today.

Breathe... God is with you.

____

____

____

____

____

____

____

____

____

____

____

____

____

____

Day 6: Patience in Chaos

Scripture: *"Be completely humble and gentle; be patient, bearing with one another in love." – Ephesians 4:2*

Hey Mommy…Patience can feel impossible some days. The house is loud. The kids are arguing. Someone spilled something. Again. And your to-do list is staring at you like it's judging your life choices. In those moments, patience feels very far away. But patience isn't something you manufacture. It's something God grows in you.

Motherhood will stretch you. It will expose triggers you didn't know you had. It will refine you in ways nothing else can. And while that stretching is uncomfortable, it's also holy work.

Before you react today, pause. ***Take a breath.***

Invite the Holy Spirit into that specific moment. Patience isn't about never correcting; it's about correcting with love. It means you respond instead of exploding. It means you remember that little hearts are still learning just like you. You won't get it right every time, but every time you choose gentleness over frustration, you are shaping the atmosphere in your home.

God is patient with you. Let that patience overflow onto your children.

Prayer: Lord, grow patience in me. When I feel overwhelmed… slow me down. Help me respond with love instead of reacting in frustration. In Jesus' name, Amen.

Mouth Moment
I walk in humility, gentleness, and patience.
I choose love in every interaction today.

Breathe... God is with you.

Mommy Moment: What situations tend to test my patience the most? How can I prepare my heart before those moments happen?

Day 7: A Heart of Gratitude

Scripture: *Give thanks in all circumstances…" – 1 Thessalonians 5:18*

Mama… It's easy to notice what's hard.

The mess. The exhaustion. The chaos. But gratitude shifts everything. Gratitude doesn't ignore the struggle; it just refuses to let the struggle have the final word.

In the middle of tantrums, tiny hands are reaching for you. In the middle of laundry piles, there are clothes belonging to people you prayed for. In the middle of sleepless nights, there is a child who feels safest in your arms.

When you start looking for blessings, you'll find them everywhere. The giggles. The spontaneous hugs. The "I love you, Mommy." The quiet moments when they fall asleep beside you. Gratitude turns survival mode into a sacred perspective. It softens your heart. It steadies your spirit.

Today, instead of focusing on what's overwhelming, ask yourself: *What is beautiful right now?* It might be small. But small things matter.

Prayer: Heavenly Father, help me see the beauty in this season. Teach me to choose gratitude, even on hard days. In Jesus' name, Amen.

Mouth Moment
I give thanks in all circumstances.
My heart is filled with gratitude today.

Mommy Moment: List five small blessings from today that I might normally overlook.

Day 8: Be Still and Know

Scripture: *"Be still, and know that I am God." – Psalm 46:10*

Stillness feels unrealistic in motherhood. There's always something needing attention. Someone is calling your name. Something unfinished. But stillness isn't about silence in your home, it's about quiet in your heart. Even in the noise, you can pause internally.

Close your eyes for a moment. Take one deep breath. Whisper, "God, You are in control." You don't have to hold everything together. You don't have to solve every problem. You don't have to control every outcome. Being still is choosing trust over striving. When anxiety starts climbing, stillness reminds you: He is God. Not you. And that is freeing.

You are responsible for being faithful, not being in control.

So today, build in tiny moments of stillness, even if it's just sixty seconds before getting out of the car, even if it's in the shower, even if it's after everyone goes to bed. Your soul needs quiet. And God meets you there.

Prayer: Lord, calm my racing thoughts. Help me remember that You are in control. Teach me how to rest in You, even in the noise. Amen.

Mouth Moment
I will be still and trust God.
He is in control, and I am at peace.

Breathe... God is with you.

Mommy Moment: What makes it hard for me to slow down? What would intentional stillness look like in my current season?

Day 9: Cast Your Cares

Scripture: *"Cast all your anxiety on Him because He cares for you." – 1 Peter 5:7*

Motherhood comes with worry. You worry about their health. Their friendships. Their future. Their choices. The weight of responsibility can feel heavy. But God never intended for you to carry it alone.

The word "cast" is active. It means to throw it. Release it. Don't gently set it down and pick it back up five minutes later. Actually… give it to Him. Picture yourself placing each fear into God's hands. The diagnosis. The school issue. The financial concern. The behavioral struggle.

He cares deeply! Not just about your children. About you. You don't have to pretend you're not anxious. You must refuse to carry anxiety by yourself. Every time worry resurfaces, pray again. Release it again. Trust again. You are not the ultimate protector of your family. God is. And His arms are stronger than yours.

Prayer: Father, I give You my fears. Help me release control and trust that You love my children even more than I do. Amen.

Mouth Moment
I release every worry to God.
He cares for me, and I am not alone.

Mommy Moment: What specific worries keep replaying in my mind? Can I write them down and consciously surrender them to God?

Day 10: Persistent Prayer

Scripture: *"Pray continually." – 1 Thessalonians 5:17*

Prayers don't have to be long and poetic. It can be whispered over a sink full of dishes. Spoken softly while rocking a baby. Prayed silently in a school parking lot. Prayer is a conversation. You don't need perfect words. You need an open heart.

Talk to God about everything. Silly things. The frustrating things. The overwhelming things. The beautiful things. Invite Him into your daily rhythm.

"Lord, give me patience right now." "Help me respond well." "Thank You for that sweet moment." "I don't know what to do here."

When prayer becomes constant, peace remains steady. It helps keep your heart in harmony, softens your reactions, and elevates your focus. You're never bothering God; He takes joy in hearing your voice.

Make prayer your lifeline, not your last resort.

Prayer: Lord, teach me to talk to You throughout my day. Let prayer become as natural as breathing. Amen.

Mouth Moment
I stay connected to God in prayer.
My heart remains in constant
communication with Him.

Mommy Moment: When during my day do I forget to pray? How can I build simple prayer reminders into my routine?

Day 11: God Hears You

Scripture: *"Then you will call on me and come and pray to me, and I will listen to you." – Jeremiah 29:12*

Have you ever prayed and wondered if anyone was listening? You whisper desperate prayers at night. You cry out in the car. You ask for help in the middle of chaos. And sometimes… it feels quiet.

But God is not silent because He is absent. He is attentive. He hears the exhausted sigh. He hears the frustrated whisper. He hears the tearful "I can't do this."

You may feel overlooked by the world, but you are never ignored by God. He doesn't roll His eyes at your repeated prayers. He doesn't grow impatient with your emotions. He leans in. Even when answers take time, His listening never ceases.

Your prayers are not bouncing off the ceiling. They are landing in the heart of a Father who loves you deeply. Keep praying. Keep calling. Keep trusting.

He hears you, Mommy.

Prayer: Lord, thank You for hearing every word I pray. Even when I don't see answers yet, help me trust that You are listening and working. Amen.

Mouth Moment
I call on God, and He hears me.
My prayers are received, and I am not ignored.

Day 12: Ask, Seek, Knock

Scripture: *"Ask and it will be given to you; seek and you will find; knock and the door will be opened to you." – Matthew 7:7*

Sometimes we hesitate to ask God for things. We think, "This is too small." Or "Other people have bigger problems." Or "I should be able to handle this." But Jesus tells you to ask. To seek. To knock. Boldly.

God is not bothered by your needs. He invites them. Ask for patience. Ask for wisdom.

Ask for energy. Ask for peace. Ask for help in that specific situation with your child. He delights in providing for His daughters. And sometimes the greatest gift isn't the answer; it's the closeness that comes from seeking Him.

Don't hold back today. Bring everything. Nothing is too small for a God who numbers the hairs on your head.

Prayer: Jesus, help me come to You confidently. Teach me to ask without fear and trust Your timing with the answers. Amen.

Mouth Moment
I ask, seek, and knock in faith.
God responds, and doors are opening for me.

Mommy Moment: What have I been hesitant to ask God for? What would bold faith look like in this season?

Day 13: The Peace of God

Scripture: *"Do not be anxious about anything... And the peace of God... will guard your hearts and your minds in Christ Jesus." – Philippians 4:6–7*

Anxiety can sneak in quietly. You start thinking about the future. You replay conversations.
You imagine worst-case scenarios. Before you know it, your heart feels heavy. But God offers something different, peace that doesn't make logical sense. Not peace because everything is perfect. Peace because He is present.

When you pray instead of panic, something shifts. Gratitude softens your worry. Surrender steadies your heart. Peace becomes the guard at the door of your mind. It doesn't mean concerns disappear. It means they don't control you. When anxious thoughts start spiraling, stop and pray! Even if it's short. "Lord, I give this to You." Do it repeatedly if needed.

His peace is not fragile. It's strong. Protective. Steady. And it's available right now.

Prayer: Father, guard my heart and mind with Your peace. When anxiety rises, remind me to surrender it to You immediately. In Jesus' name, Amen.

Mouth Moment
I will not be anxious about anything.
God's peace guards my heart and mind.

Breathe... God is with you.

Mommy Moment: What anxious thought keeps repeating in my mind? How can I replace it with prayer and gratitude?

Day 14: The Lord is Near

Scripture: *"The Lord is near to all who call on him..." – Psalm 145:18*

There are days when God feels close. And there are days when He feels distant. But feelings are not facts. This verse doesn't say He is near only when you feel spiritual. It says He is near when you call.

Call on Him while folding laundry. Call on Him during a meltdown. Call on Him when you feel discouraged. You don't have to earn His nearness. He is not pacing heaven waiting for you to be perfect. He is already beside you.

Sometimes His nearness looks like comfort. Sometimes it looks like clarity. Sometimes it looks like strength you didn't know you had. But He is always near. Motherhood can feel overwhelming, but you are never navigating it alone. Call on Him. He's closer than you think.

Prayer: Father, thank You for being near! Help me sense Your presence in ordinary moments and lean on You daily. In Jesus' name, Amen.

Mouth Moment
The Lord is near to me when I call.
I am never alone… He is right here.

Mommy Moment: When do I feel closest to God? How can I intentionally call on Him more throughout my day?

Day 15: Strength in the Lord

Scripture: *"I can do all this through him who gives me strength." – Philippians 4:13*

There are days when you feel capable. And there are days when you feel completely undone. Motherhood has a way of humbling you fast. But your strength was never meant to come from confidence in yourself. It comes from confidence in Him.

You don't have to do it all. You don't have to be it all. You don't have to hold it all together. When you feel weak, that's not the end; that's the invitation.

Lean in. God's strength shows up best in surrendered hearts. He will strengthen you to apologize when needed. To love when it's hard. To persevere when you're tired. To show up again tomorrow. You are stronger than you think, not because of you, but because of Him. And He never runs out.

Prayer: Lord, I don't want to rely on myself. Be my strength today. Empower me to be a mother with grace, courage, and love. Amen.

Mouth Moment
I can do all things through Christ.
His strength is working in me today.

Mommy Moment: Where am I trying to rely on my own strength instead of God's? What would surrender look like in that area?

Day 16 – When You Feel Invisible

Scripture: *Genesis 16:13-So she called the name of the Lord who spoke to her, "You are a God of seeing," for she said, "Truly here I have seen him who looks after me."*

Hey Mama! Have you ever felt unseen? Like you're pouring and pouring, and no one notices? The meals, the cleaning, the emotional labor, the remembering of everything for everyone?

In Genesis, Hagar called God *El Roi*, the God who sees me. Not the God who sees the finished product. Not the God who sees the polished version. The God who sees *you*… tired bun, messy kitchen, overwhelmed heart, and all.

You may feel overlooked by people, but Heaven never overlooks you.

God sees the sacrifice, the restraint, the prayers whispered over sleeping children, and the tears you wipe away before anyone walks back into the room. And here's the beautiful part: when God sees, He responds. His seeing is never passive.

Mama, you are not invisible. A faithful God witnesses you. Even when no one thanks you. Even when no one applauds you. Even when no one understands you. He sees you fully, and He stays.

Prayer: El Roi, thank You for seeing me completely. When I feel invisible, remind me that I am fully known by You. Help me rest in Your awareness of my life. In Jesus' name, Amen.

Mouth Moment
God sees me and cares for me.
I am never overlooked or forgotten.

Breathe… God is with you.

Mommy Moment: What do I wish people would notice about me? How does it change things to know God sees me? Where can I shift my focus from human validation to divine affirmation?

Day 17 – Progress, Not Perfection

Scripture: *Philippians 1:6-And I am sure of this, that he who began a good work in you will bring it to completion at the day of Jesus Christ.*

Mama… perfection is exhausting. And honestly? It was never the goal. We set impossible standards: "I'll be more patient tomorrow." "I won't raise my voice again." "I'll have it all together." Then one rough moment makes us feel like we're back at square one.

But growth is rarely linear. Philippians tells us that He who began a good work in you will carry it to completion. That means *He's still working.* You are under construction, and that's not a flaw. It's a promise.

Progress looks like:

- Apologizing faster.

- Recovering quicker.

- Recognizing triggers.

- Pausing before reacting.

That's growth. Mama, don't disqualify yourself because you're not perfect yet. Celebrate that you're not who you used to be. God isn't asking for flawlessness. He's forming faithfulness. Let Him work! Even in the messy middle.

Prayer: Lord, thank You for not being finished with me yet. Help me value progress over perfection and trust that You are completing what You started. In Jesus' name, Amen.

Mouth Moment
God is finishing what He started in me.
My life is a work in progress, by His hands.

Breathe... God is with you.

Mommy Moment: Where are you expecting perfection instead of celebrating progress?

Day 18 – The Power of Your Words

Scripture: *Proverbs 18:21-Death and life are in the power of the tongue, and those who love it will eat its fruits.*

Mama… your words matter more than you think. The tone. The reactions. The labels you speak over your children and yourself. Proverbs says life and death are in the power of the tongue. That's not poetic exaggeration. That's spiritual reality. Your voice is shaping atmospheres.

When you say, "You are capable." "You are loved." "We will figure this out." You are building identity. And Mama… this includes how you talk to yourself. If you wouldn't say it to your child, don't say it to yourself. Words can wound. But they can also water growth.

This isn't about being fake-positive. It's about being intentional. Before you respond today, pause and ask: Will this build or break?

Your words carry authority in your home. Use them gently. Use them wisely.

Prayer: Father, guard my mouth and guide my tone. Help my words bring life, correction with love, and encouragement that builds confidence. In Jesus' name, Amen.

Mouth Moment
I speak life over myself and my family.
My words produce fruit and power today.

Breathe… God is with you.

Mommy Moment: What kind of tone has filled your home lately?

Day 19 – When You're Running on Empty

Scripture: *Psalm 23:3-He restores my soul. He leads me in paths of righteousness for his name's sake.*

Mommy… be honest. Are you tired in your bones? Not just sleepy, but soul-weary? Psalm 23 says He restores my soul. Not "He scolds my exhaustion." Not "He ignores my burnout." He restores. Sometimes we keep pushing because stopping feels irresponsible. But running on empty doesn't serve anyone in the long term.

You can't pour from an empty pitcher. Restoration starts with awareness. Admit you're depleted. That's not weakness… that's wisdom.

Then ask: What is draining me? What is refilling me? Where have I neglected myself?

God restores through: Quiet time. Honest prayer. Healthy boundaries. Trusted community.

Mama, depletion is a signal, not a sentence. Let the Shepherd lead you beside still waters again.

Prayer: Good Shepherd, restore my soul. Show me where I need to slow down and receive Your care. Lead me back to still waters. In Jesus' name, Amen.

Mouth Moment
God restores my soul.
He leads me on the right path today.

Breathe… God is with you.

Mommy Moment: What has been draining you most lately?

Day 20 – You Are Allowed to Grow

Scripture: *2 Corinthians 3:18-And we all, with unveiled face, beholding the glory of the Lord, are being transformed into the same image from one degree of glory to another. For this comes from the Lord who is the Spirit.*

Mama… hear this clearly. You are allowed to evolve. Motherhood changes you. Life changes you. Healing changes you. And sometimes people expect you to remain the same version of yourself forever.

But Scripture says we are transformed from glory to glory. Growth doesn't mean you've abandoned who you were. It means God is revealing who you're becoming.

You may outgrow:

- Certain mindsets.

- Certain habits.

- Even certain relationships.

And that's okay. Growth can feel lonely, but stagnation feels heavier. Mama, you are allowed to pursue healing. You are allowed to seek therapy. You are allowed to dream again. You are allowed to become more whole. Don't shrink to stay comfortable for others. Let God stretch you into new strength.

Prayer: Lord, continue transforming me. Give me the courage to embrace growth, even when it's uncomfortable. Help me trust who You're shaping me to be. Amen.

Mouth Moment
I am being transformed by God daily.
I am growing from glory to glory.

Breathe… God is with you.

Mommy Moment: Where do you feel God stretching you right now?

Day 21 – Love Is Patient, Even with Yourself

Scripture: *"Love is patient and kind; love does not envy or boast; it is not arrogant or rude."* – 1 Corinthians 13:4 (ESV)

Hey, Mama… We quote this verse at weddings. We teach it to our children. We hang it on our walls. But have you ever applied it to yourself? Patience isn't just something you extend to your kids when they spill the milk again. It's something you extend to yourself when you mess up for the third time this week.

When you lose your temper, forget something important, or fall short of your own expectations, God's love for you does not rush. It is not irritated. It does not roll its eyes at your growth. He is patient with you. So why are you so harsh with yourself? Growth takes time. Healing takes time. Learning new habits takes time. You are allowed to be in process.

Mama… speak to yourself the way you would speak to your daughter. You are not failing. You are learning. Grace upon grace is available to you today.

Prayer: God, help me to be patient with myself. Let me rest in Your grace and remember that I am a work in progress. In Jesus' name, Amen.

Mouth Moment
I walk in love that is patient and kind.
I choose humility and grace today.

Day 22 – The Spirit Will Guide You

Scripture: *"But the fruit of the Spirit is love, joy, peace, patience, kindness, goodness, faithfulness."* – Galatians 5:22 (ESV)

Mama… Patience isn't something you squeeze out by willpower. It's fruit. And fruit grows when it stays connected to the vine. You don't have to wake up and manufacture patience on your own. You simply stay connected to the Holy Spirit and let Him cultivate it in you.

When you feel yourself getting frustrated… pause. Whisper a quick prayer. Invite Him into that exact moment. The Spirit doesn't just guide you in big life decisions. He guides you in tone. In timing. In restraint. You are not parenting alone.

The more you lean into Him, the more His fruit shows up in your reactions. Mama… this journey is not powered by your strength. It is sustained by His presence.

Prayer: Holy Spirit, guide me in patience and kindness. Let Your presence shape my heart and actions. In Jesus' name, Amen.

Mouth Moment
The fruit of the Spirit lives in me.
I walk in love, joy, peace, and patience.

Mommy Moment: In what situations do you struggle most with patience?

Day 23 – Be Still and Know

Scripture: *"Be still and know that I am God." –* Psalm 46:10 (ESV)

Mama… Stillness feels unrealistic sometimes. The house is loud. The schedule is full. Your mind is running ahead to tomorrow. But stillness isn't about silence around you, it's about surrender within you.

You might not have a whole hour to yourself, but even sixty seconds can help. Close your eyes, take a deep breath, then exhale slowly. Remember, God is in control, not you. There's no need to manage every outcome, fix every problem, or be a perfect mom.

He is already in tomorrow. He is already working in your child's heart. He is already handling what's keeping you up at night.

Mama… pause today. Let your nervous system settle. Let your faith rise. Stillness is not laziness. It is trust.

Prayer: Lord, help me to be still in Your presence. Remind me that You are in control, and I can rest in You. In Jesus' name, Amen.

Mouth Moment
I will be still and know God is in control.
My heart is calm, and my mind is at peace.

Breathe… God is with you.

Mommy Moment: What is making it hard for you to slow down right now?

Day 24 – Love Is Patient

Scripture: *"Love is patient, love is kind..."* – 1 Corinthians 13:4 (NIV)

Mama… Patience can feel impossible on the third meltdown of the day. The laundry isn't done.
Dinner isn't ready. Someone is crying, maybe you. But patience is not passive. It's powerful.

When you pause instead of snapping…
When you breathe instead of yelling…
When you respond instead of reacting…

You are reflecting Christ. Patience doesn't mean you never correct. It means you correct with love. Your children are learning what love looks like by watching you. And yes, you will mess this up sometimes. We all do. But every new moment is another opportunity to try again.

Take a deep breath today. Ask God to fill you with His patience.

You don't have to do this perfectly… just prayerfully.

Prayer: Lord, help me to be patient today. When challenges arise, let me respond with love instead of frustration. Teach me to reflect Your kindness and grace. In Jesus' name, Amen.

Mouth Moment
I choose love in every moment today.
My words and actions reflect God's love.

Mommy Moment: When is your patience tested the most?

Day 25 – Love Is Kind

Scripture: *"Be kind and compassionate to one another…"* – Ephesians 4:32 (NIV)

Hey Mama… Kindness changes atmospheres. A soft tone. A gentle touch. A simple "I understand." Kindness doesn't mean you ignore behavior. It means you address it without tearing the heart down. And here's something important: kindness applies to you, too.

The way you talk to yourself sets the emotional climate of your home. If your inner dialogue is harsh, it will spill outward. Kindness is strength under control. Did you hear that? Kindness is strength under control!

Today, choose softness in your words. Choose compassion in correction. Choose grace in frustration.

Your home can feel different when kindness leads.

Prayer: Father, help me to be kind in my words, actions, and attitude. Let my home be filled with Your love through acts of kindness. In Jesus' name, Amen.

Mouth Moment
I am kind and compassionate.
I choose grace in every interaction today.

Breathe... God is with you.

Day 26 – Love Never Fails

Scripture: *"Love never fails."* – 1 Corinthians 13:8 (NIV)

Mama… There will be days when you question everything. Am I doing enough? Did I handle that correctly? Am I messing this up? Motherhood has a way of magnifying self-doubt.

But here's the truth anchored in Scripture: love never fails. Not performance. Not perfection. Not Pinterest-level parenting. Love!

You will have imperfect moments. You will have tired reactions. You will have days you wish you could redo. But when your heart posture is love, real, sacrificial, trying-again love… it carries more weight than your mistakes.

Love covers a harsh tone when you apologize. Love heals a tense moment when you hug. Love rebuilds a connection after correction. God's love toward you is constant. And as you root your motherhood in Him, that love flows through you.

Mama… if you lead with love, you are not failing.

Prayer: Lord, thank You for Your unfailing love. Help me trust that when I lead with love, I am walking in what matters most. In Jesus' name, Amen.

Mouth Moment
Love never fails.
I lead with love in all I do.

Day 27 – Love Forgives

Scripture: *"Bear with each other and forgive one another..."* – Colossians 3:13 (NIV)

Mama… Forgiveness is not optional in motherhood. It is essential. You'll need to forgive: Your children. Your spouse. Yourself. Little offenses pile up quickly in a home. Eye rolls. Sharp tones. Forgotten responsibilities. Exhausted reactions.

If we don't release them, resentment builds quietly. But forgiveness keeps your heart soft. Forgiveness doesn't mean ignoring behavior. It means refusing to let bitterness take root. And sometimes the hardest person to forgive is yourself.

You replay the moment and cringe at your tone, wishing you could undo it. But God doesn't dwell on yesterday — so why are you holding onto it?

Mama, release it. Apologize when needed. Teach your children what grace looks like in action. And move forward without dragging shame behind you. A forgiving heart creates a peaceful home.

Prayer: Father, help me extend forgiveness freely to others and to myself. Keep my heart tender and free from bitterness. In Jesus' name, Amen.

Mouth Moment
I choose forgiveness and extend grace.
I release offense and walk in love.

Mommy Moment: Is there anything you're holding on to that needs to be released?

Day 28 – Love Casts Out Fear

Scripture: *"There is no fear in love. But perfect love drives out fear…"* – 1 John 4:18 (NIV)

Mama… Fear sneaks in quietly. Fear of the future. Fear of failing. Fear of something happening to your children. It can sit heavy in your chest if you let it. But God says His perfect love drives out fear. That means fear doesn't get to stay where love is rooted.

You don't have to pretend you're never afraid. You bring your fear into the presence of love.

When anxious thoughts start spiraling, pause and remind yourself:

God loves my children more than I do.
He sees what I cannot see.
He holds what I cannot control.

Fear shrinks when trust grows.

Mama… you are not raising your children alone. Heaven is invested in their story.

Let love be louder than worry today.

Prayer: Lord, I surrender my fears to You. Let Your perfect love quiet my anxious thoughts and anchor me in trust. In Jesus' name, Amen.

Mouth Moment
There is no fear in love.
God's perfect love drives out all fear.

Breathe… God is with you.

Mommy Moment: What fear has been occupying your thoughts lately?

Day 29 – Love Serves

Scripture: *"Through love serve one another..."* – Galatians 5:13 (ESV)

Mama... Motherhood is service in its purest form.

You serve when you cook. You serve when you listen. You serve when you wake up in the middle of the night. But service can start to feel heavy when it feels unnoticed.

Here's the shift: you are not serving only your family — you are serving through love.

When you change your perspective from "I have to" to "I get to," something softens inside.

Service rooted in love reflects Jesus.

And no act is too small.

Folding laundry can be worship.
Packing lunches can be ministry.
Driving the carpool can be sacred.

Mama... your daily sacrifices matter.

Serve, yes — but also rest. Service is beautiful when it flows from love, not obligation.

Prayer: Jesus, help me to serve with a joyful heart. Let my daily acts of love reflect Your love for me. In Jesus' name, Amen.

Mouth Moment
I serve others through love.
My actions reflect God's heart today.

Breathe... God is with you.

Mommy Moment: How do you view the daily tasks of motherhood?

____

____

____

____

____

____

____

____

____

____

____

____

____

____

Day 30 – Love Is a Choice

Scripture: *"Above all, put on love, which binds everything together in perfect unity."* – Colossians 3:14 (ESV)

Mama… Love is not just a feeling. It's a decision.

Some days it flows naturally. Other days, it requires intention.

When you're tired.
When you're overstimulated.
When everyone needs something at once.

Love is choosing gentleness anyway.
Choosing connection anyway.
Choosing grace anyway.

"Put on love" means it's something you intentionally wear.

Just like you get dressed each morning, you can clothe yourself in love before the day begins.

It won't mean the day is easy. But it will mean your responses are rooted in something deeper.

Mama… choose love today — not because it's easy, but because it's powerful.

Prayer: Lord, help me to choose love today. Let it be the foundation of all I say and do, even when it takes effort. Amen.

Mouth Moment
I put on love today.
Love leads me and holds everything together.

Breathe... God is with you.

Mommy Moment: What does choosing love look like in a hard moment?

Day 31 – God's Love Is Unfailing

Scripture: *"Give thanks to the Lord, for He is good; His love endures forever."* –
Psalm 136:1 (NIV)

Before we talk about your strength, let's anchor in something first… His love
never runs out.

Not on your worst day. Not after your sharpest tone. Not when you feel
completely inadequate.

His love endures forever.

That means when you wake up tired, His love is still steady.
When your patience feels thin, His love is still thick.
When you question yourself, His love remains confident over you.

You are mothering from a place of being loved — not from a place of striving to
earn it. And when you truly rest in that, something shifts.

You stop parenting under pressure.
You stop leading from fear.
You stop measuring your worth by outcomes.

Mama… you are sustained by an unfailing love. And that love empowers you to
love your children well.

Prayer: Father, thank You that Your love never fails and never fades. Help me rest
in that truth and parent from a place of security, not striving. In Jesus' name,
Amen.

Mouth Moment
God is good, and His love endures forever.
My heart is filled with gratitude today.

Breathe… God is with you.

____

____

____

____

____

____

____

____

____

____

____

____

____

____

____

____

Day 32 – Kind Words Heal

Scripture: *"Gracious words are a honeycomb, sweet to the soul and healing to the bones."* – Proverbs 16:24

Your words carry weight!!! They can build confidence, or chip away at it. They can calm chaos or ignite it.

And let's be honest, when you're tired, it's easy to let frustration leak out in your tone. But Scripture reminds us that gracious words heal.

Your child may not remember every meal you cook — but they will remember how you made them feel. Kind words don't mean you avoid correction. They mean correction comes wrapped in dignity.

And don't forget … you need gracious words too. The way you speak to yourself sets the emotional climate in your home. If your inner voice is harsh, everything feels heavier.

Mama… pause before responding today. Choose words that sweeten the atmosphere.

Healing can start in your mouth.

Prayer: Lord, help me speak words that heal. Guard my tone and let my voice bring life, encouragement, and strength into my home. Amen.

Mouth Moment
My words are kind and life-giving.
I speak healing and encouragement today.

Day 33 – Love in Action

Scripture: *"Dear children, let us not love with words or speech but with actions and in truth."* – 1 John 3:18

Mom,

Love isn't just something we say, it's something we show.

It's in the way you sit and listen, even when you're busy.
It's in the way you show up to the game, the recital, the hard conversation.
It's in the small sacrifices no one claps for.

Your actions preach louder than your words.

And here's the good news… You don't have to perform grand gestures. Small acts consistently shape hearts.

Packing a favorite snack.
Leaving a note.
Offering a hug after discipline.

These are seeds.

Mama… your daily actions are forming memories and a sense of security. You are building trust brick by brick.

Love in action creates safety.

Prayer: Father, help my love be visible. Show me how to love not just in words, but in action and truth. In Jesus' name, Amen.

Mouth Moment
I show love through my actions.
I live in truth and love daily.

Breathe... God is with you.

Mommy Moment: What small act of love could have a big impact today?

Day 34 – The Strength of Kindness

Scripture: *"Be completely humble and gentle; be patient, bearing with one another in love."* – Ephesians 4:2

Kindness is not weakness.

It takes strength to remain gentle when everything in you wants to snap. It takes strength to stay patient after you've answered the same question five times. It takes strength to lead calmly when the house feels chaotic.

Gentleness is controlled strength. And God equips you with that strength daily.

You don't have to dominate your home to lead it. You can lead with steadiness, humility, and love. And when you feel yourself reaching your limit, that's your cue to pause, not explode.

Mama… strong doesn't mean loud. Strong can be soft.

Your calm presence can anchor an entire room.

Prayer: God, give me strength wrapped in gentleness. Help me lead with humility and patience, even when I feel stretched thin. In Jesus' name, Amen.

Mouth Moment
I walk in humility, gentleness, and patience.
I choose love in every moment today.

Breathe... God is with you.

Mommy Moment: What situations test your gentleness the most?

Day 35 – Sowing Seeds of Kindness

Scripture: *"A generous person will prosper; whoever refreshes others will be refreshed."* – Proverbs 11:25

Some days feel repetitive. You pour and pour… and don't always see immediate results.

But every act of kindness is a seed.

Every encouraging word.
Every patient response.
Every bedtime prayer.

Seeds take time to grow.

You may not see the fruit today, but one day you will.

A confident adult who remembers your reassurance.
A compassionate heart shaped by your example.
A resilient spirit, strengthened by your patience.

Keep sowing! And here's the promise… when you refresh others, you will be refreshed. God has a way of refilling what you pour out in obedience.

Mama… don't underestimate the power of consistent kindness.

Prayer: Lord, help me continue to sow kindness even when growth feels slow. Refresh my spirit as I pour into my family. In Jesus' name, Amen.

Mouth Moment
I refresh others with love and generosity.
I am refreshed as I give.

Breathe... God is with you.

Mommy Moment: Where do you feel like you're not seeing results yet?

____

____

____

____

____

____

____

____

____

____

____

____

____

____

____

____

Day 36 – Reset, Don't Replay

Scripture: *"Forget the former things; do not dwell on the past. See, I am doing a new thing!" – Isaiah 43:18–19*

Mama… how many times have you replayed the same moment in your mind?

The tone you wish you could take back. The reaction that came out too quickly. The moment you wish you could redo. Wishing you had said it differently, handled it better, and been more patient.

But replaying the moment won't redeem it. God never asked you to relive it. He invites you to release it. The enemy wants you stuck in replay. God wants you to walk in renewal.

Yes, acknowledge the moment. Yes, grow from it. Yes, apologize if needed. But then… reset.

You are not called to carry guilt from moment to moment. You are called to walk in grace and growth. Every day… every hour… sometimes every minute… is a fresh opportunity to begin again.

Mama, you are not defined by one hard moment. You are being shaped through many redeemed ones. So instead of replaying what went wrong… Lean into what God is doing right now.

He is not stuck in your yesterday. And you don't have to be either.

Prayer: Lord, help me never to allow my mistakes ever to hold me captive. Help me know that your grace covers me, and that I have the power to repent and move forward. In Jesus' name, Amen.

Mouth Moment
I release that which I cannot change.
I am not stuck in my past… I am growing forward.

Breathe… God is with you.

Mommy Moment: What moment have I been replaying in my mind? What would it look like to truly release it and choose a fresh start today?

Day 37 – The Power of Your Presence

Scripture: *"The Lord bless you and keep you…"* – Numbers 6:24

Sometimes we think our children need grand gestures.

Big vacations. Perfect holidays. Over-the-top experiences. But what they really crave is presence.

Your listening ear.
Your laughter.
Your sitting beside them when they talk about something that seems small to you but feels big to them. Presence says, "You matter."

You don't have to be perfect. You just must be available.

Even five intentional minutes of eye contact, no phone, no distraction… that plants security.

Your presence brings peace.
Your attention builds identity.
Your consistency creates safety.

And when you feel stretched thin, ask God to help you be fully present in the moments that matter most.

You are a blessing simply by being there.

Prayer: Father, help me to truly understand how much my presence means to those who depend on me daily. Please remove anything that would distract me from being present. In Jesus' name, Amen.

Mouth Moment
The Lord blesses and keeps me.
I am covered and protected today.

Breathe… God is with you.

Mommy Moment: Where can I be more intentionally present this week? What small adjustment could make a big difference?

Day 38 – The Joy of Giving

Scripture: *"It is more blessed to give than to receive."* – Acts 20:35

Mama, one of the most beautiful parts of motherhood, is giving.

Your time, your energy, your love. Pouring yourself out can feel exhausting, but there's hidden joy in it. When you give with a cheerful heart, you're not just serving your children; you're reflecting the heart of God.

Sometimes giving doesn't look like something huge.
It's making that extra snack even when you're tired.
It's pausing to hug a tearful child instead of checking your phone.
It's whispering encouragement over a school project instead of rushing through chores.

When you give with love, you're teaching your children something powerful: life is about others, not just yourself. And here's the secret… they notice. Even if they don't say it today, they are learning compassion, patience, and generosity from watching you.

Your small acts of giving matter. They matter more than you think. They are not wasted. They are planting seeds that will bear fruit for years to come.

Remember to give to yourself as well. Rest, prayer, and God's presence are gifts that refill your cup so you can keep pouring out love without running dry.

Prayer: Lord, help me to consistently spend time in your presence, which is an amazing gift, so that I can, in turn, be the gift that my children need me to be. Help me teach them that life is not just about them. In Jesus' name, Amen.

Mouth Moment
I find joy in giving.
I am blessed as I bless others.

Breathe… God is with you.

Mommy Moment: What is one small way I can give today that will make a difference? How can I intentionally give joyfully, not out of obligation?

Day 39 – Clothed in Kindness

Scripture: *"Therefore, as God's chosen people, holy and dearly loved, clothe yourselves with compassion, kindness, humility, gentleness, and patience." –* Colossians 3:12

Motherhood can be messy! Literally and figuratively! But today, let's focus on what we "wear" on the inside.

Clothing yourself in kindness is like choosing your outfit for the day. It's intentional. It's deliberate. You can't control every circumstance, but you *can* control how you respond.

Even when your patience is tested, when the laundry pile grows, or the toddler screams at the checkout line, choose kindness. Not because your children will always notice, but because God notices.

Kindness is powerful. It softens hearts. It calms tensions. It models Christ to your family in ways words sometimes can't. And here's the good news… You don't have to conjure it alone. Ask God to wrap you in His compassion, to give you gentleness when you feel harshness rising. His strength becomes your kindness.

Today, your actions, words, and even your tone can speak louder than any lesson. Clothe yourself with love, patience, and humility; it's a choice, a daily wardrobe of the heart.

Prayer: Lord, thank You for loving and choosing me. Help me to walk in kindness, patience, and gentleness today. When frustration rises, remind me to respond with grace. Let my life reflect Your love. In Jesus' name, Amen.

Mouth Moment
I am chosen, loved, and set apart.
I walk in compassion, kindness, and patience.

Breathe... God is with you.

Mommy Moment: How can I intentionally "wear" kindness today? Are there moments I anticipate needing extra patience or gentleness?

____

____

____

____

____

____

____

____

____

____

____

____

____

____

____

____

Day 40 – Rest in His Grace

Scripture: *"Come to me, all you who are weary and burdened, and I will give you rest."* – Matthew 11:28

Momma, you've poured so much into others—meals, hugs, lessons, bedtime routines. You've given love tirelessly. But don't forget—you also need to rest.

Rest isn't just sleep (though that helps!). It's allowing God's grace to refill your heart and mind. It's letting go of perfection. It's breathing deeply and remembering that His strength carries you when you feel empty.

The weight of responsibility can be heavy. Some days it may feel like too much. But grace is sufficient. God doesn't expect you to do it all alone or perfectly. He just asks you to come to Him, weary hands lifted, and receive His peace.

Pause for a moment. Close your eyes. Feel God's arms holding you. He sees every sacrifice, every late night, every tear. He calls you to rest—not out of laziness, but to restore your spirit so you can continue loving well.

You are enough, even when your list isn't done. You are loved, even when patience runs thin. And you are strengthened through God's grace, which never runs out.

Prayer: Lord, I come to You weary and in need of rest. Help me to release the pressure to do everything perfectly. Fill me with Your peace and restore my strength. Remind me that you hold me. In Jesus' name, Amen.

Mouth Moment
I come to God and find rest.
My burdens are lifted, and I am restored.

Breathe... God is with you.

Mommy Moment: Where in my day can I pause and rest in God's grace? How can I remind myself that I don't have to carry everything alone?

____

____

____

____

____

____

____

____

____

____

____

____

____

____

____

Day 41 – God Goes Before You

Scripture: *"The Lord himself goes before you and will be with you; he will never leave you nor forsake you. Do not be afraid; do not be discouraged."* – Deuteronomy 31:8

Momma, some days motherhood feels overwhelming. Responsibilities, schedules, and the unknown can feel heavy. But here's the beautiful truth: God goes before you. He's already prepared the way. He's already worked out the details you can't see yet.

When you feel unsure, take a deep breath and rest in His promise. You don't have to have all the answers. You don't have to control everything. God has gone ahead to clear the path and will walk beside you every step of the way.

Fear and doubt may whisper in your ear, but God's presence is stronger. He will guide, protect, and sustain you, even when life feels unpredictable. Lean into Him today, knowing you are never walking alone.

Prayer: Lord, thank You for going before me and walking beside me. Help me to trust You when I don't have all the answers. Remove fear and fill me with peace and confidence in You. Remind me that I am never alone. In Jesus' name, Amen.

Mouth Moment
God goes before me and stays with me.
I will not fear or be discouraged.

Breathe... God is with you.

Mommy Moment: What areas of my life or motherhood do I need to trust God to go before me? How can I release fear and rest in His guidance today?

Day 42 – Strength Comes from the Lord

Scripture: *"So do not fear, for I am with you; do not be dismayed, for I am your God. I will strengthen you and help you; I will uphold you with my righteous right hand."* – Isaiah 41:10

Mama, exhaustion is real. There are days when your body is tired, your heart is heavy, and your patience is stretched thin. But remember: your strength doesn't come from you—it comes from the Lord.

When you feel weak, He is strong. When your energy is gone, He provides what you need. When you feel like giving up, He will hold you up with His mighty hand. You don't have to do this alone.

Lean into Him. Pray for His strength. Ask Him to renew your spirit. God sees your efforts, your love, and your sacrifice. His power is perfect in your weakness, and His grace will sustain you through every challenge.

Prayer: Lord, thank You for being my strength when I feel weak. Help me to rely on You and not my own ability. Renew my energy and uphold me with Your mighty hand. Help me to remember that I am sustained by You. In Jesus' name, Amen.

Mouth Moment
I will not fear—God is with me.
He strengthens, helps, and upholds me.

Breathe... God is with you.

Day 43 – Be Strong and Courageous

Scripture: *"Have I not commanded you? Be strong and courageous. Do not be afraid; do not be discouraged, for the Lord your God will be with you wherever you go."* – Joshua 1:9

Fear can sneak in, Mama—fear of mistakes, fear of judgment, fear of the unknown. But God's command is clear: be strong and courageous. Why? Because He is with you. Always.

Courage isn't the absence of fear—it's trusting God despite it. When challenges arise, when your patience is tested, when your heart feels heavy, remember He hasn't left your side. God equips you with the courage you need for today.

So, take a step forward in faith. Speak words of encouragement to your children. Face difficult moments with confidence. Lead your family with strength, knowing God goes before you and stands beside you.

Prayer: Lord, help me to be strong and courageous today. When fear tries to rise, remind me that You are with me. Give me the strength to move forward in faith and not doubt. Fill my heart with confidence in You. In Jesus' name, Amen.

Mouth Moment
I am strong and courageous.
God is with me wherever I go.

Breathe... God is with you.

Mommy Moment: What area of my life or motherhood requires courage today? How can I rely on God to walk with me through it?

____

____

____

____

____

____

____

____

____

____

____

____

____

____

____

____

____

Day 44 – Do Everything with Love

Scripture: *"Be on your guard; stand firm in the faith; be courageous; be strong. Do everything in love."* – 1 Corinthians 16:13-14

Strength is important, but strength without love can feel empty. Mama, your patience, your discipline, and your authority are all most powerful when they are rooted in love.

Even on the hardest days, when tantrums, chores, or exhaustion challenge you, let love guide your actions. Speak with grace, discipline with kindness, and lead with a heart full of God's love. This love is what shapes your children's hearts and teaches them how to live with compassion.

Love doesn't always come naturally; it's a choice. But every time you choose love, you're modeling Christ for your family. Your home becomes a place of grace, understanding, and security.

Prayer: Lord, help me to do everything with love today. Guide my words, my actions, and my responses with Your grace. When I feel overwhelmed, remind me to choose love. Let my life reflect Your heart. In Jesus' name, Amen.

Mouth Moment
I stand firm in my faith.
I am strong, courageous,
and led by love.

Mommy Moment: How can I let love guide my words and actions today, even in challenging moments? Where might I need to choose love over frustration?

Day 45 – Trust in His Plans

Scripture: *"Trust in the Lord with all your heart and lean not on your own understanding; in all your ways submit to him, and he will make your paths straight."* – Proverbs 3:5-6

Momma, it's natural to worry about what's ahead—school schedules, family needs, finances, and your children's future. However, God invites you to trust Him. His plans are greater than your fears, and His timing is flawless.

When uncertainty knocks, surrender your worries to God. Trust that He is directing your steps, even when the path seems unclear. Lean into His wisdom instead of your own understanding.

Today, I choose faith over fear and trust over worry. His ways are higher than yours, and His love is constant. When you place your hope in Him, you can walk confidently, knowing He is in control and that your family is held in His hands.

Prayer: Lord, help me to do everything with love today. Guide my words, my actions, and my responses with Your grace. When I feel overwhelmed, allow me to choose love. Let my life reflect Your heart. In Jesus' name, Amen.

Mouth Moment
I trust God with all my heart.
He is directing my path today.

Breathe... God is with you.

Mommy Moment: Where am I struggling to trust God's plan? How can I intentionally surrender control and lean on His understanding today?

Day 46 – His Grace is Sufficient

Scripture: *"But he said to me, 'My grace is sufficient for you, for my power is made perfect in weakness.'"* – 2 Corinthians 12:9

Mama, you don't have to be perfect. You're human, and motherhood will show you that your strength has limits. But here's the good news: God's grace fills in every gap where you feel weak.

When patience wears thin, when mistakes happen, when the days feel too long—His grace is enough. His power shines brightest in your moments of weakness, covering your shortcomings and enabling you to keep going.

Lean on Him. Invite His grace into your day. Accept that it's okay to not have it all together. God sees your heart, your effort, and your love, and He provides what you need exactly when you need it.

Prayer: Lord, thank You that Your grace is enough for me. Help me release the need to be perfect and to lean on You. Fill the places where I feel weak with Your strength. Remind me that I am covered by Your grace. In Jesus' name, Amen.

Mouth Moment
God's grace is sufficient for me.
His power is working in my weakness.

Breathe... God is with you.

Day 47 – You Are Equipped

Scripture: *"May he equip you with everything good for doing his will."* –
Hebrews 13:21

Momma, God hasn't left you unprepared. Every tool you need to love, teach, and guide your children has already been given to you. You are equipped for this journey, even when it doesn't feel that way.

When self-doubt creeps in, remember that God sees your potential and has placed all the resources, wisdom, and strength inside you to fulfill your calling. You don't have to compare yourself to anyone else; you have exactly what you need.

Take confidence in the knowledge that God equips you day by day. Trust Him, lean on Him, and step forward boldly, knowing you're fully prepared to handle the challenges of motherhood.

Prayer: Lord, thank You for equipping me for this journey. Help me to trust what You've placed inside of me. When doubt rises, help me to know that I am prepared and capable through You. Give me confidence to walk boldly in my calling. In Jesus' name, Amen.

Mouth Moment
God equips me for His will.
I have everything I need to do well.

Breathe... God is with you.

Mommy Moment: In what areas do I feel unequipped? How can I trust God to provide what I need for today?

Day 48 – Do Not Be Anxious

Scripture: *"Do not be anxious about anything, but in every situation, by prayer and petition, with thanksgiving, present your requests to God."* – Philippians 4:6-7

Mama, anxiety can sneak in quietly, whispering worries about school, schedules, or your children's futures. But God calls you to lay every worry at His feet. Through prayer, petition, and gratitude, He invites you to trade anxiety for His perfect peace.

Take a deep breath. Present your concerns to God. Allow His peace to settle over your heart and mind. Even amid uncertainty, He is in control. Trust that He is listening and working for your good. You don't have to carry the weight alone.

Prayer: Lord, I give every worry and concern to You today. Help me to trust You instead of holding onto anxiety. Fill my heart and mind with Your peace. Remind me that You are in control. In Jesus' name, Amen.

Mouth Moment
I release anxiety and choose prayer.
God's peace fills my heart today.

Breathe... God is with you.

Mommy Moment: What worries am I holding onto today? How can I bring them to God in prayer and trust Him to handle them?

Day 49 – The Lord is Your Strength

Scripture: *"The Lord is my strength and my shield; my heart trusts in him, and he helps me."* – Psalm 28:7

Momma, exhaustion can hit hard. There are moments when your body is tired, your mind is overwhelmed, and your patience feels stretched thin. But even in those moments, God remains your source of strength. He is not just watching from a distance—He is actively helping you, covering you, and holding you up.

When your energy fades and your patience wears thin, remember that He is your shield and your helper. You don't have to push through on your own. Your heart can rest in Him, trusting that He will give you exactly what you need for each moment.

Allow His strength to replenish you. Pause, breathe, and lean into His presence. Let Him refill what has been poured out. God is ready to lift you up, guide your steps, and protect your family. You are never alone in the work you do, and you are never without help.

Prayer: Lord, thank You for being my strength and my shield. When I feel tired and overwhelmed, help me to lean on You. Renew my energy and strengthen my heart for today. Remind me that I am supported and sustained by You. In Jesus' name, Amen.

Mouth Moment
The Lord is my strength and my shield.
My heart trusts Him, and He helps me.

Breathe... God is with you.

Mommy Moment: Where do I feel drained today? How can I lean on God to give me strength and renew my spirit?

Day 50 – Persevere with Endurance

Scripture: *"Let us run with perseverance the race marked out for us."* – Hebrews 12:1

Momma, motherhood isn't a sprint—it's a marathon. Some days feel long, and some nights feel endless. There are moments when you may feel like slowing down or even giving up. But God has given you the endurance to keep going. He has equipped you for this race, and He is with you every step of the way.

Perseverance isn't just about showing up… It's about continuing in faith, even when the finish line isn't in sight. It's choosing to keep loving, keep teaching, and keep pressing forward, even when you feel tired.

Take heart in the small victories, the hug after a rough morning, the bedtime story, the loving correction. These moments matter more than you realize. Each step, though tiring, is shaping something beautiful in your children and in you.

So, keep going, Momma. God sees every effort, every sacrifice, and every act of love. And when you feel like your strength is fading, He will renew you so you can continue running your race with endurance.

Prayer: Lord, thank You for giving me the strength to keep going. Help me to persevere, even when I feel tired or discouraged. Renew my endurance and remind me that my efforts matter. Give me grace to continue this race with faith and love. In Jesus' name, Amen.

Mouth Moment
I run my race with perseverance.
I will not give up…
I keep moving forward.

Breathe… God is with you.

Mommy Moment: In what areas do I feel like giving up? How can I lean on God to persevere with patience and endurance today?

____

____

____

____

____

____

____

____

____

____

____

____

____

____

____

____

DAY 51 – God Will Strengthen You

Scripture: *"But the Lord is faithful, and he will strengthen you and protect you from the evil one." – 2 Thessalonians 3:3*

Momma, it's heavy, right? Sometimes it seems like every day brings a new challenge… emotional, physical, spiritual. But here's the good news: God is faithful. He sees your struggles, your sleepless nights, your doubts, and He promises to strengthen you. You don't have to rely on your own power; His strength is more than enough. Today, when you feel weary, pause and let God's strength renew your spirit. Trust that He's not just watching, you are His beloved, and He is actively working to carry you through every trial.

Even in the moments when you feel unseen or unappreciated, God is still present, covering you with His grace. The strength you need will meet you right where you are, not where you think you should be. Every tear, every prayer whispered in exhaustion, and every act of love you give does not go unnoticed by Him.

So, take a deep breath, Momma. You are not failing! You are being sustained. God is fortifying you from the inside out, equipping you for this very season. And when you can't find the words to pray, rest in His presence, knowing that His faithfulness never runs dry and His protection never fails.

Prayer: Father, thank You for Your faithfulness. Strengthen me today in ways I cannot even measure. Protect my heart, my mind, and my family, and remind me that Your power is sufficient for every challenge I face. In Jesus' name, Amen.

Mouth Moment
God is faithful to me.
He strengthens and protects
me daily.

Breathe... God is with you.

Mommy Moment: Where do I feel weak or overwhelmed today? How can I invite God's strength into that space?

DAY 52 – Strength for the Weary

Scripture: *"But those who hope in the Lord will renew their strength. They will soar on wings like eagles; they will run and not grow weary; they will walk and not be faint." – Isaiah 40:31*

Mom, I see you. You've been running! Physically, emotionally, spiritually. Some days feel endless, and the weight of responsibility feels heavier than you can carry. But God promises renewal. He doesn't just restore a little energy; He gives you strength to soar, to run without giving up, to walk without fainting. Your hope in Him is the fuel that refreshes your heart and renews your spirit. Lean into Him, take a deep breath, and let His strength lift you above the chaos.

Even when progress feels slow, remember… walking is still forward movement. God is not rushing you; He is sustaining you step by step. There is grace for the running seasons, and there is grace for the walking seasons, too.

So don't be discouraged if today doesn't feel like soaring. Your strength is being renewed even now, in the quiet moments, in the pauses, in the prayers you whisper under your breath. Keep your hope anchored in Him, Mom—you are being carried, strengthened, and prepared for more than you can see.

Prayer:
Father, renew my strength today. When I feel like I can't go on, lift me and remind me that I can do all things through You. Help me to place my hope fully in Your power. In Jesus' name, Amen.

Mouth Moment
My strength is renewed in the Lord.
I rise, run, and walk without fainting.

Breathe… God is with you.

Mommy Moment: Which areas of my life feel draining right now? How can I rely on God to renew my strength today?

Day 53 – God's Grace is Enough

Scripture: *"My grace is sufficient for you, for my power is made perfect in weakness."* – 2 Corinthians 12:9

Momma, perfection is not the goal… God's grace is. When you feel like you're not enough, His strength steps in. Your love, though imperfect, is more than sufficient when it's rooted in Him.

Rest in that truth today: grace covers every misstep and empowers you to keep moving forward.

In the moments when you feel stretched thin, overwhelmed, or unsure, remember, your weakness is not a setback, it's an invitation, an invitation for God's power to show up in ways you could never manufacture on your own.

You don't have to have it all together to be a good mom. You must stay connected to the One who holds you together. His grace fills the gaps, strengthens your heart, and meets you right in the middle of your need.

So… breathe, Momma. You are covered. You are carried. And right here, in your weakness, God's power is shining the brightest.

Prayer: Lord, help me to rest in the truth of Your word today. Help me to truly understand that Your grace covers every single one of my steps. Help me to consistently invite you into every situation and moment in my life, especially when I feel inadequate. In Jesus' name, Amen.

Mouth Moment
God's grace is sufficient for me.
His power is perfected in my weakness.

Breathe... God is with you.

Mommy Moment: Where do I feel inadequate? How can I invite God's grace to fill those moments?

Day 54 – You Are Not Alone

Scripture: *"The Lord himself goes before you and will be with you; he will never leave you nor forsake you. Do not be afraid; do not be discouraged." –* Deuteronomy 31:8

Some days, motherhood feels isolating. But God is walking with you, ahead of you, and beside you. You are never alone, even when the challenges seem overwhelming.

Trust His presence and take comfort in His companionship.

Even in the quiet moments, when no one sees your sacrifices, when the house is still, and your heart feels full yet tired… God is right there with you. He goes before you into every unknown, every decision, every new season, already making a way.

You don't have to carry fear or discouragement, because His presence replaces both with peace. When you feel uncertain, remind yourself: God has already stepped into this moment before you did.

So, take courage, Momma. You are not navigating this journey by yourself. The One who called you to motherhood is the same One who walks with you through it, faithfully, gently, and every single step of the way.

Prayer: Lord, thank You for always being with me. When I feel alone, remind me of Your presence. Replace my fear with Your peace and my doubt with Your comfort. Help me to walk confidently, knowing You are right beside me.
In Jesus' name, Amen.

Mouth Moment
God goes before me and stays with me.
I will not fear or be discouraged.

Breathe… God is with you.

Mommy Moment: When do I feel alone or unsupported? How can I rest in God's presence today?

Day 55 – Peace in the Chaos

Scripture: *"Peace I leave with you; my peace I give you. I do not give to you as the world gives. Do not let your hearts be troubled and do not be afraid."* – John 14:27

Mama, life is noisy and messy, but Jesus offers a peace that is unshakable. Even in chaos, you can pause and breathe, knowing that His peace surrounds you.

Let His calm guide your heart today.

His peace isn't dependent on quiet rooms or perfect moments—it meets you right in the middle of the noise, the to-do lists, and the unexpected interruptions. It settles your heart when everything around you feels unsettled.

When anxiety tries to creep in, gently remind yourself that His peace has already been given to you. You don't have to chase it—you just must receive it.

So slow down, Mama. Take a deep breath and release what you cannot control. Allow His peace to quiet your thoughts, steady your emotions, and remind you that no matter what today holds, you are held by Him.

Prayer: Lord, thank You for Your peace that surrounds me. Help me to release what I cannot control and rest in You. Calm my mind, steady my heart, and quiet every anxious thought. Remind me that I am held in Your peace today.
In Jesus' name, Amen.

Mouth Moment
God's peace fills my heart.
I am calm, steady, and unafraid.

Breathe... God is with you.

Mommy Moment: Where do I need God's peace in my day? How can I let His presence calm my heart amidst chaos?

____

____

____

____

____

____

____

____

____

____

____

____

____

Day 56 – God Sees Your Hard Work

Scripture: *"Let us not become weary in doing good, for at the proper time we will reap a harvest if we do not give up." – Galatians 6:9*

Mama, every little act of love, every meal, hug, bedtime story, and correction matters. God sees it all. Your faithfulness is never unnoticed. Keep going; your efforts are planting seeds that will bear fruit.

Even on the days when it feels repetitive or unappreciated, God is working beneath the surface. What you are sowing in patience, love, and consistency is taking root in ways you may not yet see.

Don't let discouragement convince you that it isn't making a difference. Growth takes time, and the harvest doesn't come overnight… but it is coming.

So, stay faithful, Mama. Keep showing up, keep loving, keep pouring in. In due season, you will see the fruit of your labor, and it will be worth every moment you choose not to give up.

And even before the harvest appears, God is shaping your heart, strengthening your character, and building something lasting within your family. Nothing you do in love is ever wasted.

Prayer: Lord, thank You that my efforts are seen by You. Help me to remain faithful, even when I don't see immediate results. Strengthen my heart when I feel discouraged. Remind me that my labor in love is never in vain. In Jesus' name, Amen.

Mouth Moment
I will not grow weary in doing good.
My harvest is coming in due season.

Breathe… God is with you.

Mommy Moment: Where do I feel my work is unseen? How can I trust that God sees every small effort?

Day 57 – The Lord is Your Helper

Scripture: *"God is our refuge and strength, an ever-present help in trouble." –* Psalm 46:1

When life gets hard, remember, Momma: you don't have to do this alone. God is your refuge and strength. Call on Him, and He will provide help, comfort, and guidance in every challenge.

He is neither distant nor delayed—He is ever-present. In the midst of your hardest moments, your busiest days, and your quiet cries, He is there. You can run to Him, rest in Him, and be renewed by Him.

When you feel overwhelmed, let Him be your safe place. When you feel weak, let Him be your strength. When you don't know what to do next, let Him guide your steps.

So, pause today, Momma, and take refuge in His presence. You are not facing anything on your own; your help is already here, and His strength is more than enough to carry you through.

Prayer: Lord, thank You for being my refuge and my strength. Help me run to You when I feel overwhelmed. Guide my steps and be my help in every moment. Remind me that I am never facing anything alone. In Jesus' name, Amen.

Mouth Moment
God is my refuge and my strength.
He is my ever-present help.

Mommy Moment: What challenges am I facing today? How can I rely on God to be my helper and guide?

Day 58 – God's Mercies are New Every Morning

Scripture: *"Because of the Lord's great love, we are not consumed, for his compassions never fail. They are new every morning; great is your faithfulness." –* Lamentations 3:22-23

No matter how yesterday went, today is fresh. God offers new mercies, new strength, and new patience. Each morning is a gift, a chance to start anew, wrapped in His love.

Yesterday's mistakes, frustrations, and exhaustion do not define you today. God's mercy meets you right where you are, not where you wish you had been. His compassion covers every brief moment, every tired response, and every time you felt you fell short.

You don't need to carry yesterday into today. Release it, Momma. God has already set aside new grace for this very moment.

Rise with hope. Walk in His mercy. And remember… each new morning is proof that His faithfulness toward you never runs out. And even if today starts slow or imperfect, His mercy is already there, ready to meet you with grace.

Prayer: Lord, thank You for new mercies today. Help me to release yesterday and embrace Your grace. Renew my strength, my patience, and my perspective. Remind me that Your faithfulness covers me. In Jesus' name, Amen.

Mouth Moment
God's mercies are new for me today.
I am covered by His faithfulness.

Breathe… God is with you.

Mommy Moment: What mistakes or burdens from yesterday do I need to release? How can I embrace God's new mercies today?

Day 59 – You Are Doing Holy Work

Scripture: *"Whatever you do, work at it with all your heart, as working for the Lord, not for human masters."* – Colossians 3:23

Momma, motherhood is holy work. Every act of nurturing, guiding, and loving is sacred and seen by God. Your efforts hold eternal significance, even when they seem small or go unnoticed.

The meals you prepare, the lessons you teach, the prayers you whisper over your children… none of it is wasted. When you do them with love and intention, you are serving the Lord in a beautiful and powerful way.

Even on the days when there is no applause, no recognition, and no immediate results, heaven takes notice. God sees your heart, your sacrifice, and your consistency.

So, keep giving your best, Momma—not for perfection, but for purpose. What you are doing matters far beyond what you can see, and your faithfulness is making an eternal impact. And even when it feels ordinary, God is using your daily acts of love to build something extraordinary in your family.

Prayer: Lord, thank You for trusting me with this calling. Help me to serve with love and give my best each day. Remind me that my work has purpose, even when it feels unseen. Strengthen me to continue with faith and joy. In Jesus' name, Amen.

Mouth Moment
I give my best in all I do.
I work with purpose, as unto the Lord.

Mommy Moment: Where do I need affirmation that my work matters? How can I serve my family today as an act of worship to God?

Day 60 – God Chose You for This

Scripture: *"Before I formed you in the womb I knew you, before you were born, I set you apart."* – Jeremiah 1:5

You were chosen for this role as a mother. God handpicked you for your children. He has equipped you, prepared you, and walks with you every step. Trust in His plan and embrace the calling He has placed in your heart.

There is no mistake in who you are or where you are. God intentionally placed your children in your care, knowing exactly what they would need—and knowing that you would be the one to give it.

Even on the days when you question yourself, remember: God's calling comes with His covering. He doesn't assign without equipping, and He doesn't choose without sustaining.

So, walk confidently in your role, Momma. You are not just raising children, you are nurturing purpose, shaping lives, and fulfilling a divine assignment that only you were chosen to carry. And even when you feel uncertain, God's hand is still on you, guiding you and strengthening you for every moment.

Prayer: Lord, thank You for choosing me for this calling. Help me to trust that I am equipped and prepared by You. When doubt comes, remind me that You are sustaining me. Give me confidence to walk boldly in my purpose. In Jesus' name, Amen.

Mouth Moment
I am chosen and set apart by God.
My life has purpose and meaning.

Breathe... God is with you.

Mommy Moment: What insecurities do I need to surrender to God? How can I embrace the calling He has given me as a mother?

About the Author

Shamarian "Shaye" Lister is a woman of faith, an associate pastor, a wife, and a devoted mother of five who understands both the beauty and the challenges of motherhood. Her journey into motherhood didn't come the way she once imagined, but through God's grace, marriage, and adoption, she now walks confidently in the calling God placed on her life.

With a full-time career in law enforcement, along with balancing family and entrepreneurship, Shaye knows what it feels like to be stretched, overwhelmed, and in need of a moment to breathe. Her experiences, both the joyful and the challenging, have strengthened her faith and deepened her dependence on God.

Through *Take A Breath, Mommy*, Shaye shares encouragement, truth, and practical moments of reflection to help other mothers pause, reset, and reconnect with God in the middle of everyday life.

Her desire is simple: to remind every mom that she is seen, supported, and strengthened by God, and that even in the busiest moments, she can take a breath and keep going.

Speak it. Believe it. Breathe again.

Take a Breath, Mommy